Keighley & Worth Valley Railway

David Mather

C000174301

© David Mather 2015

All rights reserved. No part of this publication may be reproduced, stored in a retrieval system or transmitted, in any form or by any means, electronic, mechanical, photocopying, recording or otherwise, without prior permission in writing from Silver Link Publishing Ltd.

First published in 2015

British Library Cataloguing in Publication Data

A catalogue record for this book is available from the British Library.

ISBN 978 1 85794 455 6

All photographs are the author's copyright unless otherwise credited.

Silver Link Publishing Ltd
The Trundle
Ringstead Road
Great Addington
Kettering
Northants NN14 4BW

Tel/Fax: 01536 330588

email: sales@nostalgiacollection.com
Website: www.nostalgiacollection.com

Printed and bound in the Czech Republic

Title page: **OAKWORTH** In this scene from the 1950s at Oakworth station, a former Midland Railway 0-4-4 tank pauses with its train. *N. E. Stead, KWVR Archives*

Contents

Acknowledgments

I would like to offer my sincere thanks to the several photographers who have generously allowed me to use their work in this book, together with those fellow enthusiasts who have given so freely of their time, knowledge and advice during its production. Special mention must go to Rick Ward for his help, particularly in securing the use of the photographs taken by his late friend Douglas Todd of Leeds, and to Geoff Cryer and Phil Horton for very kindly granting permission to use their images within these pages. I would particularly like to add my thanks to Paul Brunt, archivist to the railway, for his invaluable assistance. Gratitude is also due to the unsung heroes – the small army of volunteers whose enthusiasm helps to make visiting the Worth Valley Railway such a pleasure. Without them, this treasure would cease to exist.

About the author

David Mather has been a lifelong railway enthusiast, from the steam days of the 1950s and '60s through to the present. Born and brought up in industrial Lancashire, his local 'patch' was centred on Bolton, with its busy shed, coded 26C (later 9K), its routes to Manchester and Blackburn and, of course, to the West Coast Main Line. Following his graduation from Birmingham University and a time spent teaching in the West Midlands, he moved back to the North of England, albeit to the other side of the Pennines. After taking early retirement from his successful career in science teaching in the historic railway city of York, he now devotes more time to his leisure interests, prominent among which had always been railways and photography. The digital revolution afforded the opportunity to bring his large stock of negatives and slides back to life and, in association with Silver Link Publishing, this led to a series of railway titles starting with *Running out of Steam: The photographic diary of a teenage railway enthusiast, 1966-68* (published in 2010 with a Foreword by Ian Allan). This was quickly followed by *Riding the Settle & Carlisle* (2011), *Great Britain's Heritage Railways* (2012) and *The Railways of York* (2014). Further works are in preparation.

Introduction

On Saturday 13 April 1867 a special train carrying local dignitaries departed from Keighley station, marking the opening of the Keighley & Worth Valley Railway, though the engine's first attempt to climb the severely curved gradient out of the station proved embarrassingly unsuccessful and the train had to be set back beyond the platform to enable it to take a run at the bank. An inauspicious start you might think, but two days later the public passenger-carrying service began with six trains daily (just two on Sundays) operating to Oxenhope, almost 5 miles along the line. From 1 July the line was opened for freight traffic, and until 1 July 1881 it was operated by the independent Keighley & Worth Valley Railway Company. It was then taken over by the Midland Railway Company, whereupon considerable further investment was made to improve the branch, including the rebuilding of the station at Keighley. Locomotives responsible for the services in those early years probably included Johnson's Class 1F 0-6-0 tanks introduced from 1878, which operated on both passenger and freight trains in the area, several being allocated to nearby Manningham shed, Bradford, from where they worked until after the Grouping of 1923.

With the introduction of push-pull working on the branch from the early 1930s, Johnson's 0-6-0 tank locos were displaced by his Class 1P 0-4-4 tanks, introduced from 1881. At the same time responsibility for providing motive power for

Visiting the Keighley & Worth Valley Railway

The heritage railways continue to attract and inspire, and the Worth Valley Railway, with its rugged scenery and challenging gradients, is at the forefront of today's thriving preservation movement. Its variety of traction and rolling stock and the ever-friendly welcome of its staff make each visit a joy that has led the author and many more like him to come back for more.

Sat-nav postcodes for K&WVR stations:

Keighley	BD21 4HP
Ingrow	BD21 5AV
Damems	BD22 7AR
Oakworth	BD22 0DZ
Haworth	BD22 8NJ
Oxenhope	BD22 9JJ

OXENHOPE station on 1 January 1962, the last day of British Railways passenger services. *F. W. Smith, KWVR Archives*

Keighley shed transferred from Manningham to Skipton depot, which provided 0-4-4Ts as well as three of Johnson's more powerful Class 3F 0-6-0s, which had been introduced from 1885.

In 1934 Keighley's allocation from Skipton amounted to seven locos – one 0-6-0T, three 0-4-4Ts and three 3Fs – but by the early 1950s this had been reduced to three, the Worth Valley branch passenger engine, the branch freight engine and the yard pilot, the identities of the locos being changed on a weekly basis to allow maintenance to be carried out at the parent depot.

As had been the case back in 1867, the sharp climb out of Keighley station continued to test the engines and their crews to the full, so much so that the branch goods would start well back in the yard and rush the bank in spectacular style. Even so, the indignity of an engine stalling with a heavy load was not uncommon; it would then have to set back and try again. At holiday times excursions to the Lancashire coast would start from Oxenhope, often with a Horwich 'Crab' 2-6-0 in charge, but even these would make heavy weather of the return climb.

As the 1960s approached the threat of closure was real, even before the 1963 Beeching Report, prompting a series of economy measures that included the closure of Damems station, said to have been the smallest station on the Midland Railway, followed by that of the signal boxes at Oakworth and Haworth Goods Yard. Keighley shed was transferred back to being a sub-shed of Manningham, as Bradford and Keighley were now incorporated into the North Eastern Region of BR, while Skipton was still part of the London Midland Region. Staffing economies were also introduced, but to no avail. Passenger services over the branch ceased on 1 January 1962, followed by freight workings on 17 June. Freight over the former Great Northern branch line from Keighley to Ingrow East continued to operate for another three years, but when that too ended the GN Junction signal box was rapidly reduced to ruins by vandals and the line was soon lifted.

Left: **HAWORTH** The abandoned goods yard at Haworth before the K&WVRPS moved in. *Jack Wild, KWVR Archives*

Right: **OAKWORTH** During the early days of the embryonic preservation society, ex-LMS 3F No 43586 pauses at Oakworth with the 'Worth Valley Special' on 23 June 1962. *F. W. Smith, KWVR Archives*

K&WVR beginnings

Almost immediately following the withdrawal of the passenger service, the Keighley & Worth Valley Railway Preservation Society (K&WVRPS) was formed with the object of reopening the line for passenger traffic, and Haworth station was rented to serve as the society's headquarters, museum site and depot. Being located near the vast industrial conurbation of West Yorkshire, the preservation scheme was ideally placed to attract large numbers of visitors eager to witness steam's return to this 5-mile line set in the heart of the Pennines, running as it does on steep gradients from industrial Keighley to the moorland towns of Haworth, home of the Brontës, and nearby Oxenhope. Much needed to be done before passengers could be carried once more, and the enthusiastic volunteers wasted no time in getting to grips with the work.

On 29 June 1968, after six years of hard work, many delays and repeated frustrations, Platform 4 of Keighley station was the location for the first reopening to public traffic of a preserved standard gauge branch line since the official re-inauguration of the Bluebell Railway in August 1960. At about 2.30pm, the platform

Above: **INGROW WEST:** Ingrow West station on 13 September 1965. *KWVR Archives*

Left: **KEIGHLEY** No 41241 heads a work train in the 1960s at Great Northern Junction, when the double track and derelict signal box were still in situ. *W. H. Foster, KWVR Archives*

Left: **KEIGHLEY** The Lord Mayor of Keighley cuts the ribbon prior to the departure of the 'Re-opening Special' from Keighley station on 29 June 1968. *KWVR Archives*

Below right: **KEIGHLEY** Crowds line the trackside as the 'Re-opening Special' blasts out of Keighley and attacks the challenging climb up the Worth Valley towards Oxenhope. *Geoff Cryer*

Below: **OXENHOPE** The 'Re-opening Special' has arrived at Oxenhope to be greeted by throngs of well-wishers. *K. Roberts, KWVR Archives*

decorated with bunting, the Mayor of Keighley, assisted by the Mayoress, cut the tape and drank a toast to the success of the railway. The guests then boarded the special train, which consisted of two ex-Metropolitan Railway coaches, one ex-LMS coach, one ex-SR coach and the two Pullman Cars *Zena* (1st Class) and *Lorna* (2nd Class), for the long-awaited journey to Oxenhope. Proudly carrying the headboard 'Worth Valley Railway Re-opening Special', Ivatt Class 2 2-6-2T No 41241, painted in maroon and lettered 'KWVR', double-headed with an ex-SR 'USA' 0-6-0T painted 'American-style' in a brown and black livery and carrying No 72, hauling their train up the steep incline of the Worth Valley.

At Oxenhope the train was met by a brass band playing 'Congratulations', together with a throng of enthusiasts and well-wishers. By this time the preservation society had attracted a membership of more than 1,200, with full members paying a subscription of £1 per year. No permanent staff were employed and all the work was carried out by volunteers. In the railway's first season trains ran only at weekends and on Bank Holidays, and the return fare between Keighley and Oxenhope was

4 shillings for adults and 2 shillings for children. Haworth 'shed' soon became home for a growing stock of steam and diesel locomotives, diesel railbuses and coaches. Since then the railway has run steam and diesel trains not only every weekend throughout the year, but also daily through the summer months and during school holidays. Single and return fares are available from all stations, and Saver Tickets are also available.

As was expected in those early days, the Worth Valley line proved difficult to operate, due to its sharp curves and 1 in 75 average rising gradient all the way from Keighley to Oxenhope, and soon both Nos 72 and 41241 were showing signs of fatigue; the former regularly ran hot bearings while the latter just managed to finish the first season before it started to burst boiler tubes. Winter brought further problems as the company's smaller locomotives proved even more difficult to maintain. However, as time passed larger locos were obtained,

the skills and confidence of the volunteers increased, and the track and associated infrastructure was gradually transformed so that visitor numbers escalated from some 60,000 passengers in the first full year of operation to a peak of around 150,000 by the early 1980s. Early important improvements in the railway's assets included the installation of lathes, welding equipment and other necessary appliances at Haworth together with the digging of further inspection pits, the construction of new sheds and associated trackwork for storage at Oxenhope, not to mention the relaying of whole sections of the line, the renewal of bridges, rebuilding and extending of platforms and the wholesale refurbishment of the buildings themselves. Even so, a railway will not run itself, and the maintenance costs involved in continually keeping trackwork, buildings, rolling stock and bridges operational and in good repair soon began to increase dramatically from the modest £9,500 in 1970 to reach £76,000 by 1981, and still it continues to rise.

OXENHOPE Ivatt Class 2 2-6-2T No 41241 proudly carries the 'Worth Valley Railway Re-opening Special' headboard into Oxenhope station as, together with former SR 'USA' 0-6-0T No 72, it confirmed that the railway was officially open. *Geoff Cryer*

Keighley to Ingrow

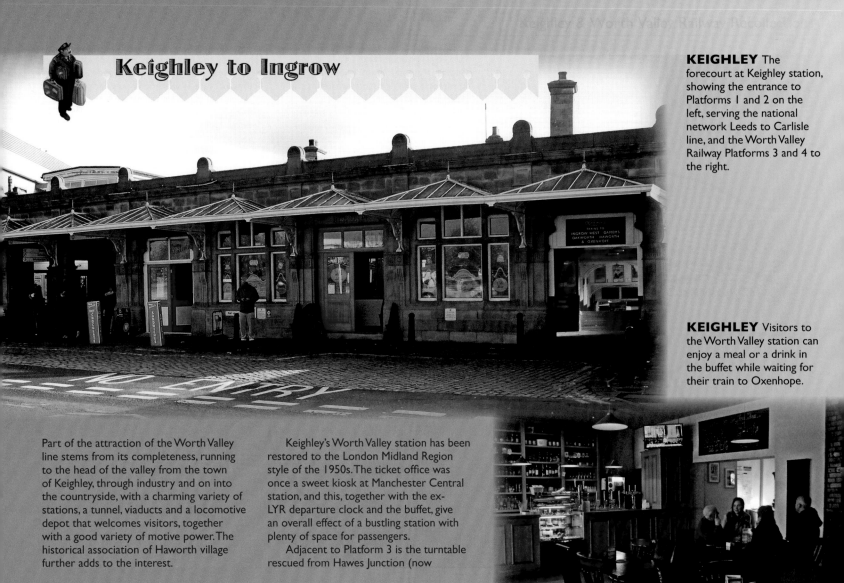

KEIGHLEY The forecourt at Keighley station, showing the entrance to Platforms 1 and 2 on the left, serving the national network Leeds to Carlisle line, and the Worth Valley Railway Platforms 3 and 4 to the right.

KEIGHLEY Visitors to the Worth Valley station can enjoy a meal or a drink in the buffet while waiting for their train to Oxenhope.

Part of the attraction of the Worth Valley line stems from its completeness, running to the head of the valley from the town of Keighley, through industry and on into the countryside, with a charming variety of stations, a tunnel, viaducts and a locomotive depot that welcomes visitors, together with a good variety of motive power. The historical association of Haworth village further adds to the interest.

Keighley's Worth Valley station has been restored to the London Midland Region style of the 1950s. The ticket office was once a sweet kiosk at Manchester Central station, and this, together with the ex-LYR departure clock and the buffet, give an overall effect of a bustling station with plenty of space for passengers.

Adjacent to Platform 3 is the turntable rescued from Hawes Junction (now

Left: **KEIGHLEY** A ramp gives access to the Worth Valley Railway's Platform 4, and at the bottom is the ticket office and beyond that, on the platform, is a well-stocked refreshment kiosk and a waiting room with a coal fire to keep passengers warm on cold winter days.

Below: **KEIGHLEY** The refreshment kiosk on Platform 4 sells a range of hot and cold drinks and snacks.

Right: **KEIGHLEY** The waiting room is comfortable and kept warm in winter.

Below: **KEIGHLEY** The carefully restored fittings give an authentic period feel to Platform 4.

Garsdale) on the Settle & Carlisle line, together with watering facilities for the ever-thirsty locos. Alongside is a pleasant picnic area, convenient for watching the trains while enjoying lunch 'al fresco'.

Below: **KEIGHLEY** Carrying a wreath of poppies in commemoration of Remembrance Day, USA Transportation Corps Class 'S160' 2-8-0 No 5820 *Big Jim*, itself a veteran of the Second World War, prepares to leave Keighley for Oxenhope on 9 November 2014.

Right: **KEIGHLEY** LMS 'Black 5' No 5305 *Alderman A. E. Draper* receives attention prior to taking the next train to Oxenhope in July 1992.

Below right: **KEIGHLEY** BR Standard Class 4MT 2-6-4T No 80002 is ready to take its train out of Keighley in October 1999. *Phil Horton*

Top left: **KEIGHLEY** LMS 4F 0-6-0 No 4422 on the turntable at Keighley in October 1995.

Left: **KEIGHLEY** Hudswell Clarke 0-6-0T No 1704 *Nunlow* is turned ready for its next duty at Keighley.

Above: **KEIGHLEY** Taking on water at Keighley in preparation for its next journey is GWR pannier tank No 5775. *Phil Horton*

Top left: **KEIGHLEY** LMS 'Jinty' 0-6-0T No 47279 waits at Keighley with a train for Oxenhope in August 1998.

Above: **KEIGHLEY** 'Black 5' No 45305 takes water at Keighley in preparation for its next run up the hill to Oxenhope.

Left: **KEIGHLEY** Former War Department 'Dub-Dee' No 90733 prepares to leave Keighley with a freight train for Haworth. This class once numbered more than 730 locomotives.

From the important town of Keighley, with its station on the 'Airedale Line', 17 miles (27km) north-west of Leeds, the Worth Valley's tracks from the completely renovated Platforms 3 and 4 curve out of the station on a severe gradient of 1 in 66, steepening further to 1 in 58 at Keighley West signal box, before easing to 1 in 114 to the site of the former Great Northern Junction signal box, where the Oxenhope branch becomes single.

KEIGHLEY Backing on to their train at Keighley in October 1999 are Manning Wardle 0-6-0 saddle tank No 1210 *Sir Berkeley* and Lancashire & Yorkshire 'Pug' No 51218 – two of the first arrivals to grace the reopened Worth Valley Railway in January 1965. *Phil Horton*

KEIGHLEY The pair are ready to be coupled to the K&WVR's vintage coaches for their trip up the valley. *Phil Horton*

Above left: **KEIGHLEY** Stanier 'Black 5' No 45305 is about to leave Keighley with a train for Oxenhope on 10 October 2014.

Above: **KEIGHLEY** It's the turn of LMS 3F 'Jinty' No 47279 to head the beautifully restored vintage coaching stock during October 1999. *Phil Horton*

Left: **KEIGHLEY** The sole survivor of the Taff Vale Railway's 'O2' Class of 0-6-2 tank locos is No 85, gracing Keighley station in May 2002. Only nine such locos were built in Glasgow and delivered to the TVR from 1899. No 85 later ran on the GWR as No 426 before being withdrawn and sold on to the National Coal Board in the 1920s. She was eventually saved for preservation and restored to her TVR livery. *Phil Horton*

Above: **KEIGHLEY** Taking up the challenge, SR Bulleid 'Pacific' No 34092 *Wells* and Ivatt 2MT 2-6-2T No 41241 storm out of Keighley station on 27 September 1980. *Geoff Cryer*

Right: **KEIGHLEY** Hauling a set of vintage coaches, former LNWR Webb 'Coal Tank' No 1054 makes a fine sight as it tackles the steep climb from Keighley on 2 May 1998. *Geoff Cryer*

Left: **KEIGHLEY** As No 1054 climbs away from Keighley, 8F No 90733 waits with a freight train.

Where the track passes under Woodhouse Road at milepost 1, a glimpse may be had of the site of the former GNR engine shed at Ingrow, long since gone but once the home of Ivatt 'C12' 4-4-2 and 'N1' 0-6-2 tanks, which operated this branch from Keighley to Bradford and Halifax, of which little evidence remains today. Ingrow West station is then reached, the 'West' having been added in BR days when Ingrow GN became Ingrow East.

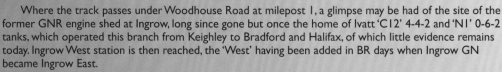

Left: **KEIGHLEY** Lancashire & Yorkshire Railway Class '25' No 52044 heads for Haworth and Oxenhope from Keighley. *Geoff Cryer*

Below left: **KEIGHLEY** BR Standard Class 2MT No 78022 sets off from Keighley. *Geoff Cryer*

Right: **KEIGHLEY** Leaving the cobbled back streets of Keighley behind, USA No 5820 *Big Jim* attacks the climb up the Worth Valley.

Below right: **TWIXT KEIGHLEY AND INGROW** Fowler 3F No 47279 climbs through the Worth Valley in June 1994. Built in 1924, the locomotive was rescued from the scrapyard after being withdrawn from service by BR in 1966.

Below: **INGROW WEST** USA 2-8-0 No 5820 arrives at Ingrow West with a train from Keighley in May 1992.

INGROW WEST Four-wheel railbus No M79960 arrives bound for Oxenhope on 9 November 2014.

KEIGHLEY Lovingly restored 'Jubilee' 4-6-0 No 45596 *Bahamas* takes water at Keighley before its next duty on 7 May 1995. *Douglas Todd/author*

INGROW WEST The ticket office.

INGROW WEST is also home to Ingrow Loco, the museum and workshop of the Bahamas Locomotive Society, and, further down the yard, the Museum of Rail Travel, both of which house fascinating collections of railway artefacts and memorabilia telling the story of the steam locomotive and those who worked with it. At the time of writing admission to both is free with a Worth Valley Railway Day Rover ticket.

INGROW WEST In addition to owning No 45596, which gives the Bahamas Preservation Society its name, Hudswell Clarke 0-6-0T No 1704 *Nunlow*, here working in the sidings at Ingrow West, is also part of the society's collection, being the first loco to be overhauled and restored by the its volunteer members in 1971.

INGROW WEST GWR 3F 0-6-0PT No 5775 and LYR Class '21' 0-4-0ST No 51218 simmer at Ingrow West on 2 May 1998. *Geoff Cryer*

From Ingrow, the line crosses the River Worth for a second time before continuing the climb to the tiny station at Damems, 2 miles out of Keighley and reputed to have been the smallest station (not a 'Halt') on the Midland Railway system. The 'request stop' station is a delight, with its signal box added from Earby, a small town historically in the West Riding of Yorkshire, whose own station was closed in 1970 when passenger trains between Colne and Skipton were withdrawn. There is a level crossing, complete with crossing-keeper's house, a waiting room and a booking office, all carefully restored to provide facilities reminiscent of those on the original station. A passing loop here is controlled from the signal box, and single-line tokens are exchanged here before trains can continue along the line.

After Damems the gradient steepens again to 1 in 60 for nearly a mile to Oakworth, where there

DAMEMS Ivatt 2-6-2T No 41241 arrives at the tiny Damems station with a train from Keighley on 1 July 1976. *Geoff Cryer*

are sidings and a goods shed, while the station itself, with its original buildings, has become something of a legend as a result of its repeated appearances among the winners of the ARPS/Ian Allan Ltd 'Best Restored Station' competition, and as the location for the filming of the 1970 film *The Railway Children*. Like most stations on the line, Oakworth is gas-lit and heated by coal fires.

OAKWORTH station has been beautifully restored to Edwardian condition, complete with cosy waiting room.

Below and right: **OAKWORTH** Goods trains are run on certain days and provide a welcome opportunity to see the railway's variety of rolling stock in action. Former Lancashire & Yorkshire Railway 0-6-0 No 52044 of 1887 vintage hauls a mixed freight into Oakworth in May 2002. *Phil Horton*

Right: **OAKWORTH** 'USA' Class 0-6-0T No 30072 from the former Southern Railway eases her train into the station.

OAKWORTH 'WD' 8F No 90733 races through the station with a non-stop 'St Valentine's Day Express' from Keighley on 14 February 2010.

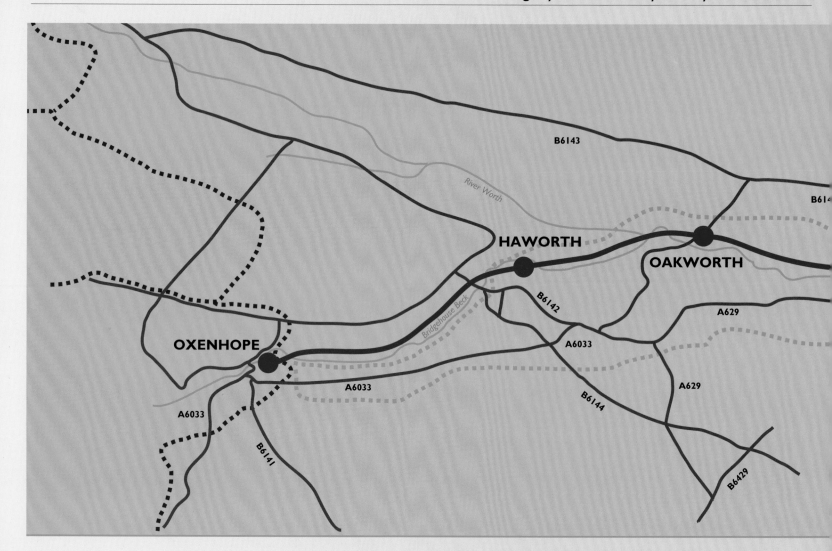

ROUTE MAP
The Keighley & Worth Valley Railway

● Stations — Main line railway

● Stations — Keighley & Worth Valley Railway

— Main roads

‑ ‑ ‑ The Worth Way

▪▪▪▪ Footpaths

B6143

A650

DAMEMS

KEIGHLEY

INGROW

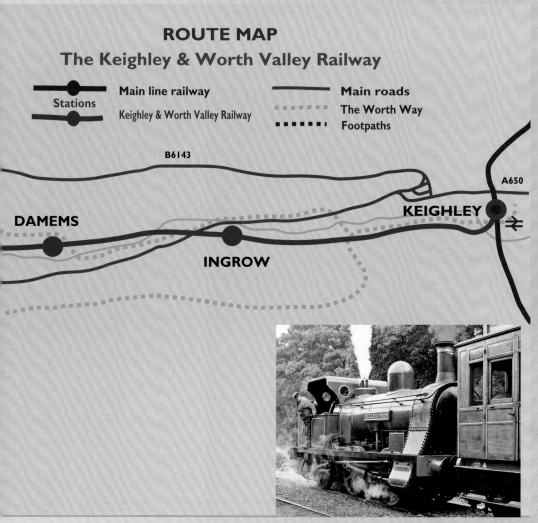

OAKWORTH The beautifully restored *Bellerophon* manoeuvres vintage coaching stock during October 1999. Herself a long-lived survivor, dating back to 1874, she is the last of only six locos ever built at the Haydock Foundry in Lancashire. *Both Phil Horton*

After the level crossing at Oakworth the line crosses the River Worth for the final time before entering the 73-yard Mytholmes Tunnel, where it leaves the Worth Valley and proceeds on towards Haworth, 3½ miles from Keighley. Haworth station, little changed over the years, has a single platform and a latticed footbridge over the line, which affords superb views of trains entering the station. The Motive Power and Civil Engineering departments are situated here, and the extensive sidings just beyond the station are used to stable much of the preservation society's rolling stock. A picnic and shed viewing area provide a convenient vantage point from which to watch the loco movements in the yard. The shop on the gas-lit platform stocks a wide range of railway items, DVDs and books, while a short walk away up the hill is the historic village of Haworth and the Brontë Parsonage Museum, located opposite the church at the top of the village.

OAKWORTH Standard 4MT No 80002 climbs out of Oakworth towards Mytholmes Tunnel on 2 May 1998.

Top left: **MYTHOLMES VIADUCT** An 0-6-0 saddle tank crosses the nearby Mytholmes Viaduct heading for Haworth. *Geoff Cryer*

Above: **HAWORTH** In keeping with all stations on the Worth Valley line, the flower beds at Haworth are lovingly tended.

Left: **HAWORTH** Approaching Haworth are two former BR locos, 2MT No 78022 and 4MT No 80002, with their train from Keighley. *Geoff Cryer*

Above: **HAWORTH** 3F 0-6-0T No 47279 of 1924 vintage pauses at a busy Haworth station. *Douglas Todd*

Above right: **HAWORTH** station footbridge is a fine vantage point from which to watch the comings and goings. 2014 saw the 65th anniversary of the original naming of ex-SR 'West Country' 4-6-2 No 34092 as *Wells*, the name it currently carries until the official renaming to *City of Wells*.

Right: **HAWORTH** station ticket office.

Top left: **HAWORTH** The well-stocked shop on Haworth station.

Left: **HAWORTH** Members of the volunteer train staff prepare for the 'off' from Haworth with their train for Keighley…

Above: **HAWORTH** … but not until the loco crew has handed over the footplate to the next shift.

Above: **HAWORTH SHED** LNER 'A4' Class No 4498 *Sir Nigel Gresley* receives attention. *Douglas Todd*

Below: **HAWORTH SHED** Class 37 diesel No 37075 and Midland Railway 4F No 43924 provide a contrast in motive power.

Above: **HAWORTH SHED** Locos in the yard at Haworth shed: this is GWR pannier tank No 5775 in the 'GN&SR' livery it carried for the film of *The Railway Children. Geoff Cryer*

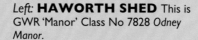

Left: **HAWORTH SHED** This is GWR 'Manor' Class No 7828 *Odney Manor.*

Above: **HAWORTH SHED** This 0-6-0 saddle tank (Works No 7289) named *Fred* was built by Robert Stephenson & Hawthorns for the War Department in 1945 and is seen here in the yard at Haworth, resplendent in its Worth Valley Railway livery. *Geoff Cryer*

Above right: **HAWORTH SHED** Designed by Fowler for the Midland Railway, 4F 0-6-0 No 43924 was built at Derby Works in 1920 and was withdrawn from service in June 1965. One of the fortunate few to be purchased for preservation, it is seen here looking splendid outside Haworth shed in October 2014.

Right: **HAWORTH SHED** Stanier 8F 2-8-0 No 48431 simmers gently at Haworth. Once numbering some 850 examples, members of this class of powerful locomotives were for many years an everyday sight throughout the region. *Geoff Cryer*

HAWORTH SHED Locos photographed in the yard at Haworth on 16 September 1989 included 'USA' 3F 0-6-0T No 30072, built in 1942 to a US Army Transportation Corps design and purchased by the Southern Railway in 1946, Taff Valley Railway 'O2' Class 0-6-2T No 85, dating back to 1899, and Southern Railway 'West Country' Class 4-6-2 No 34092 *City of Wells. Phil Horton*

Haworth to Oxenhope

Still climbing, the line leaves Haworth past the sheds on a testing gradient of 1 in 68 to run through attractive, more open scenery with gentle curves for the last mile towards the terminus at Oxenhope, where further sidings and an engine run-round loop are located beside the single platform. The neat and tidy station buildings and platform extension at the northern end of the village have been greatly enhanced since the early days of preservation.

HAWORTH USA 2-8-0 No 5820 storms away from Haworth past the engine sheds on the final leg of the journey to Oxenhope on 9 November 2014.

Above: **TWIXT HAWORTH AND OXENHOPE** On 2 May 1998 LNWR 'Coal Tank' No 1054 pilots GWR pannier tank No 5775 with a train of vintage coaches between Haworth and Oxenhope. *Geoff Cryer*

Right (2): **OXENHOPE** Now going about their regular duties, the two pioneering locos from the line's reopening are seen at Oxenhope running round their trains in preparation for the return journey. *Both Geoff Cryer*

OXENHOPE Passengers photograph 'Black 5' No 45305 as it prepares to run round its train on 10 October 2014.

Special events and visiting locomotives

Every month throughout the year, visitors to the Keighley & Worth Valley Railway can enjoy a variety of special events and unique experiences, including lunchtime dining or afternoon tea aboard the 'White Rose' Pullman dining train, guided tours of the Haworth workshops or footplate experience driver-training courses. The Beer and Music Festival in October is always a great attraction, as is the 1940s Weekend centred on Haworth.

Right: **THE JUBILEE BAR** The Jubilee is a converted BR Mark I Open Corridor coach painted in mock-Pullman livery to complement the Pullman carriages of the 'White Rose' dining train to which it is usually attached. *Paul Brunt, KWVR Archives*

Left: Named to commemorate the Queen's Silver Jubilee in 1977, the coach has been fitted with an authentic bar salvaged from a public house in Leeds, and now offers the perfect venue for parties requiring their own private bar.

Also available to hire for that special occasion are the railway's Lancashire & Yorkshire Railway Club Car of 1912 vintage, now fully restored and featuring real leather seating in its hand-crafted interior, and the Restaurant Car – the oldest Mark I coach in preservation – fully carpeted and beautifully upholstered, perfect for a private buffet lunch or family function. For details please visit the website at www.kwvr.co.uk. *Paul Brunt, KWVR Archives*

A Day Out with Thomas and Friends

Come and meet Thomas the Tank Engine and his friends as they pull their special trains up and down the valley, with the 'Fat Controller' on hand to make sure all the engines behave themselves!

Both Douglas Todd

KWVR Archives

St Valentine's Day – always a 'Special' occasion

Why not celebrate St Valentine's Day in style with a romantic trip behind a steam loco and relive the 'golden age of steam' as you are transported through the beautiful Yorkshire countryside?

Right: It's St Valentine's Day 2010 and 'WD' 8F 2-8-0 No 90733 hauls a heavy special train through the countryside between Haworth and Oxenhope.

OXENHOPE On the same day, LMS 2MT No 41241 rolls into Oxenhope station carrying a wreath of St Valentine's Day flowers.

Santa Specials

Christmas would hardly be complete without a visit from Santa, and what better way to meet him than on board his special steam train? Festive cheer and a present for the children help make this a day to be remembered.

HAWORTH Ivatt 2MT No 41241 heads a 'Santa Special' at Haworth. *KWVR Archives*

Celebrating the first 40 years

OXENHOPE On 29 June 2008 – the 40th anniversary of the reopening of the Worth Valley Railway – the crew of the Ivatt pose together with the Lord Mayors of Keighley and Bradford and honoured guests after arriving with the 'Re-opening Special' re-run. *Keith Preston, KWVR Archives*

Visiting locomotives

The ease of transfer between the Worth Valley line and the national network means that visiting locos are regularly able to grace the society's tracks, and as a result a great variety of 'guests' make a welcome appearance throughout the year, for example during the popular Gala Weekends and the Autumn Steam Spectacular held in October.

Right: **OXENHOPE** On loan from the Great Central Railway, GNR Class 'N2' 0-6-0T No 1744 takes water at Oxenhope before the return run to Keighley on 14 February 2010.

HAWORTH SHED The unique BR 8P 'Pacific' built in 1954, No 71000 *Duke of Gloucester*, poses at Haworth. *Douglas Todd*

Left: **KEIGHLEY** At Keighley we see Metropolitan Railway No 1, built in 1898 and now the only survivor of the class of seven 0-4-4T locos built for use between Baker Street and Verney Junction. *Douglas Todd*

Below left: **INGROW WEST**
Lancashire & Yorkshire Railway 'Pug' Class '21' 0-4-0ST No 51218 was built in 1901 and is still going strong. She was the first loco to arrive on the K&WVR, being delivered by road on 7 January 1965 after being purchase by the L&Y Saddletanks Fund following her withdrawal by BR in September 1964. She is seen here with a train of Metropolitan Railway carriages, beautifully restored by the Vintage Carriages Trust (VCT), which operates the Museum of Rail Travel at Ingrow West. In addition to its fine collection of carriages, the Trust also operates three steam locos: the 0-6-0 well tank *Bellerophon*, Hudswell Clarke 0-4-0 saddle tank No 402 *Lord Mayor*, and Manning Wardle 0-6-0 saddle tank No 1210 *Sir Berkeley*.
The latter, together with the first two vintage coaches for the K&WVR, were delivered on 19 January 1965, so 2015 marked the 50th anniversary of the first arrivals and of the founding of the VCT.
To celebrate, the three pioneering VCT vehicles were reunited to form special trains departing from Ingrow West station. *Geoff Cryer*

Above: **INGROW WEST** *Sir Berkeley* at Ingrow West during June 2008. *Alan Friswell*

Below: **HAWORTH SHED** Peppercorn 'A2' 'Pacific' No 60532 *Blue Peter* was an LNER design built in 1948. *Douglas Todd*

For diesel enthusiasts

The Keighley & Worth Valley Railway's 'Diesel Gala Days' are always very popular and feature a wide variety of diesel traction, including locos from the society's own stock as well as visitors from further afield.

INGROW WEST Furness Railway No 20, built in 1863 and now the flagship loco of the FR Trust, arrives at Ingrow West. *Douglas Todd*

Right: **KEIGHLEY/ HAWORTH** These two views of BR prototype English Electric 0-6-0 shunter No D226 *Vulcan* show it moving stock at Keighley in September 1989, and more recently as D0226 in Haworth yard. *Phil Horton/author*

Left: **KEIGHLEY** Class 37s Nos 37609 and 37029 work together to take their train away from Keighley. *Douglas Todd*

KEIGHLEY Class 20s in tandem: Nos 20906 and 20308 arrive at Keighley. *Douglas Todd*

KEIGHLEY Class 25 No 25059 pilots Class 50 No 50007 as they head up the valley from Keighley towards Oxenhope. *Douglas Todd*

KEIGHLEY Looking resplendent in May 2002, No 25059 waits to take a train up the hill. *Phil Horton*

Left: **INGROW WEST** The Worth Valley Railway's Class 108 DMU set, comprising Motor Composite No M51565 and Motor Brake Second No M50928, calls at Ingrow West on its journey from Oxenhope to Keighley. *Geoff Cryer*

Right: **HAWORTH** This contrasting diesel trio is made up of the Class 108 DMU set, Hudswell-Clarke 0-6-0 shunter No D2511 and English Electric Bo-Bo Type 1 No D8031. *Geoff Cryer*

Overhaul and maintenance

The continued efficiency of the railway relies heavily on the skills and expertise of the members of the K&WVR Preservation Society, who now total more than 5,000. For 50 years this army of dedicated men and women have owned, managed and operated the line. From among them, more than 530 comprise the volunteers who work tirelessly to keep the system running week in and week out, doing everything from driving and staffing the trains, restoring the rolling stock and track-laying, to selling tickets, painting, gardening and attending to the daily maintenance of all the various 'fixtures and fittings' that together make the railway the successful attraction that it now is.

The railway's Motive Power and Civil Engineering departments are situated at Haworth, and the Carriage & Wagon Maintenance Department is located at Oxenhope, and though these vital operations are not open to the public, it is here that the serious business of overhaul and repair of stock takes place.

HAWORTH SHED The engine sheds and yard at Haworth are where most of the locos are stabled, and where much of the vital maintenance work goes on 'behind the scenes'.

Below: **HAWORTH SHED** A volunteer works on restored driving wheels at Haworth. *Douglas Todd*

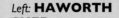

Left: **HAWORTH SHED** Whatever the weather, the volunteers work to maintain the locos in tip-top condition. Here 'West Country' Class No 34027 *Taw Valley* receives attention in a freezing Haworth yard. *Douglas Todd*

HAWORTH Manning Wardle 0-6-0ST No 1210 *Sir Berkeley* of 1891 stands in Haworth Yard during 1965, shortly after having been rescued from the cutter's torch. She had been retired from Byfield Quarries, Northamptonshire, in the early 1960s after having been transferred there from the nearby Cranford ironstone quarry, where she had inherited her name from another recently scrapped loco. On arrival at the Worth Valley Railway she was restored and took part in the BBC TV production of *The Railway Children* in 1968.

HAWORTH This loco was built in 1945 for the War Department as No 79257. She saw service in the Netherlands as No NS 4464 and on Swedish State Railways as SJ 1931, before being repatriated to the UK and restored at Haworth to become 'Austerity' 8F 2-8-0 No 90733. She is seen here at Haworth in January 1976, shortly after her return from Sweden. *Phil Horton*

HAWORTH SHED The overhaul of 2-8-0 No 90733 at Haworth has been a major project, the success of which has seen this powerful loco returned to grace the tracks once more. *Both Douglas Todd*

HAWORTH Shortly after being relocated to the Worth Valley Railway in 1965, former Lancashire & Yorkshire Railway Class '25' No 957 *Ironclad* is eased into the shed at Haworth. Built in 1887, she spent her final days working out of Wakefield loco shed before being rescued for preservation following her withdrawal from service in 1959.

HAWORTH The same engine is seen again now in her BR guise as 2F No 52044. *Geoff Cryer*

Top: **HAWORTH** *Bellerophon* stands at Haworth in July 1974. Built for the Haydock Collieries, this 0-6-0 well tank loco is the only survivor of a class of six locos built specifically to handle the heavy trains and testing gradients on the 60 miles of railway operated by the collieries. She survived until 1964 when, literally worn out, she was sent for scrapping, only to be rescued at the last minute and brought to the K&WVR. In 1981 she was purchased from the railway by the Vintage Carriages Trust for the sum of £1, and restoration work commenced. Four years later this unique loco was back in steam again, in full working order and now much in demand both here and by other heritage railways. *Geoff Cryer*

Above left: **HAWORTH** Lovingly restored, *Bellerophon* is seen again in August 1986. *Geoff Cryer*

Above left: **KEIGHLEY** A resplendent *Bellerophon* leads the charge away from Keighley station during February 1996, ably assisted by 3F tank No 47279. *Douglas Todd*

K&WVR stock

The railway's stock list of operational steam locos currently includes:

- LNWR Webb 0-6-2T 'Coal Tank' No 1054
- LMS 4F 0-6-0 No 43924
- BR 'Austerity' 2-8-0 No 90733
- USATC 'S160' Class 2-8-0 No 5820 *Big Jim*
- SR 'West Country' Class 4-6-2 No 34092 *Wells*
- Hudswell Clarke 0-6-0T No 1704 *Nunlow*
- LMS 'Black 5' 4-6-0 No 45305

Three other locos are at present working elsewhere:

- GWR '5700' Class 0-6-0PT No 5775
- LMS 'Jubilee' 5XP 4-6-0 No 45596 *Bahamas*
- LMS 'Black 5' 4-6-0 No 45212

In addition, several steam locos are currently undergoing overhaul, on static display or in storage.
The operational diesel fleet includes:

- BR 0-6-0 Class D2/12 shunter No D2511
- Mersey Docks & Harbour Board 0-6-0 shunter No 32
- BR 0-6-0 Class 08 shunter No 13336 (formerly 08266)
- BR Bo-Bo Class 25 No 25059 (formerly D5209)
- BR Bo-Bo Class 20 No 20031 (formerly D8031)
- BR 0-6-0 prototype EE shunter No D0226 *Vulcan*

- BR Class 101 DMU set Nos 51803 and 51189
- BR railbus No 79964

A Class 108 DMU set (Nos 50928 and 51565) and a second BR railbus (No 79962), as well as a diesel-mechanical 0-6-0 shunter (No 23 *Merlin*) are currently among other stock undergoing or awaiting overhaul.

The railway's rolling stock includes a fleet of 20 BR Mark 1 coaches outshopped in BR maroon livery and a fine collection of more than 20 vintage and 'special use' carriages. There are also a number of restored freight wagons and three rail-mounted cranes – a 10-ton Grafton steam permanent-way crane, a 15-ton Taylor Hubbard diesel permanent-way crane, both operational, and awaiting overhaul, and an LMS 45-ton steam breakdown crane.

By joining the Preservation Society you can become a volunteer and so help to run this exciting railway. For further details, visit the website at www. kwvr.co.uk/get-involved/membership.

INGROW WEST The breakdown crane and other stock awaiting overhaul in the yard.

The railway in film and on television

The line and its stations have been the setting for numerous period films and television productions, famously including the classic film *The Railway Children*, in which locations included Mytholmes Tunnel near Haworth and scenes around Oakworth and Haworth itself. The locos used in this production included Hudswell Clarke 0-6-0T No 31 *Hamburg*, GWR '5700' Class 0-6-0PT No 5775, LYR Class '25' 0-6-0 No 957, and GNR Class 'N2' 0-6-2T No 1744.

Above: **HAWORTH** Ebor Lane, Haworth, is the setting on 5 June 1970 for the closing scene of *The Railway Children*, as the cast wave goodbye from the engine and embankment. *KWVR Archives*

Right: **HAWORTH** Lancashire & Yorkshire Railway Class '25' No 957 at Haworth.

Above: **HAWORTH SHED** Hudswell Clarke No 31 *Hamburg* at Haworth shed. *Geoff Cryer*

Above left: **KEIGHLEY** Pannier tank No 5775, in BR livery, at Keighley. *Douglas Todd*

Below: **HAWORTH** Class 'N2' No 1744 blasts away from Haworth station.